ANF

SKEV 2/14

11 APR 2018

TRURO
8/15
CHQ

TRU

WITHDRAWN

→ CHQ 2/20 CHQ

HEL CHQ
2/16

→ TOR (CHQ)
8/23

-TRU
CHQ 11/16

SS
IOS
10/17

FREE

Why Science Hasn't Disproved Free Will

Alfred R. Mele

OXFORD
UNIVERSITY PRESS

OXFORD
UNIVERSITY PRESS

Oxford University Press is a department of the University of Oxford.
It furthers the University's objective of excellence in research, scholarship,
and education by publishing worldwide.

Oxford   New York
Auckland   Cape Town   Dar es Salaam   Hong Kong   Karachi
Kuala Lumpur   Madrid   Melbourne   Mexico City   Nairobi
New Delhi   Shanghai   Taipei   Toronto

With offices in
Argentina   Austria   Brazil   Chile   Czech Republic   France   Greece
Guatemala   Hungary   Italy   Japan   Poland   Portugal   Singapore
South Korea   Switzerland   Thailand   Turkey   Ukraine   Vietnam

Oxford is a registered trademark of Oxford University Press
in the UK and certain other countries.

Published in the United States of America by
Oxford University Press
198 Madison Avenue, New York, NY 10016

Library of Congress Cataloging-in-Publication Data
Mele, Alfred R., 1951–
    Free : why science hasn't disproved free will / Alfred R. Mele.
      pages cm
    ISBN 978-0-19-937162-4 (hardback)
    1. Free will and determinism.   I. Title.
    BJ1461.M453 2014
    123'.5—dc23
              2014006491

9 8 7 6 5 4 3 2 1
Printed in the United States of America
on acid-free paper

For my biggest fan, my father.

CONTENTS

PREFACE

Some people say that free will is an illusion. This is a book about scientific experiments that are supposed to prove those people right. I describe these experiments in ways everyone can understand, and I explain why they don't rule out the existence of free will. In fact, the illusion is that there is powerful scientific evidence for the nonexistence of free will.

As I write this preface, I'm in my final year as director of the four-year, $4.4 million Big Questions in Free Will project, funded by the John Templeton Foundation. During the course of the grant, I've continued to write for my normal academic audience, and recently I reached out to undergraduates in a small book entitled *A Dialogue on Free Will and Science* (2014). I decided it was time to try to reach out to everybody. Hence, this book. For excellent editorial assistance, I'm grateful to Julian McCaull and Lucy Randall. For helpful advice about the manuscript, I'm indebted to Michael McKenna, Mark Mele, and Manuel Vargas.

This book was made possible through the support of a grant from the John Templeton Foundation. The opinions expressed here are my own and do not necessarily reflect the views of the John Templeton Foundation. The preceding two sentences are an official report. Unofficially, I report that it's been a great pleasure to work with the good folks involved in my project at the John Templeton Foundation: Alex Arnold, John Churchill, Dan Martin, and Mike Murray. The Big Questions in Free Will project has already generated a lot of cutting-edge scientific and theoretical work on free will, and that work will inspire more good work on the topic. I am grateful to the John Templeton Foundation for their support and for the opportunity they afforded me and all the researchers to whom I was able to help direct research funds. Readers who are interested in learning about some of the fruits of the Big Questions in Free Will project should look for *Surrounding Free Will* (2015) and for a series of shows about the project in the "Closer to Truth" PBS television series.

FREE

1 | DECISIONS, DECISIONS

There are two main scientific arguments today against the existence of free will. One comes from neuroscience. Its basic claim is that all our decisions are made unconsciously and therefore not freely. The other argument comes from social psychology. This time, the basic claim is that factors of which we are unaware have such a powerful influence on our behavior that no room remains for free will.

Before I discuss the experiments on which these arguments are based, I need to say something about what "free will" means. If you were to interview passersby on the street, you would hear several different views on the topic. According to a relatively small group of people, free will is housed only in souls; it's a supernatural aspect of life. According to others, whether or not souls exist, free will doesn't depend on them. So how do *they* define free will?

Some of them will tell you that as long as you're able to make rational, informed decisions when you're not being subjected to undue force and are then able to act on the basis of some of those decisions, you have free will. (Being threatened with a loaded gun is a good example of undue force.) Others insist that something crucial must be added to these abilities: if you have free will, then alternative decisions are open to you in a deep way that I will try to shed some light on now. (I say more about this in Chapter 6.)

Sometimes you would have made an alternative decision if things had been a bit different. For example, if you had been in a slightly better mood, you might have decided to donate twenty dollars to a worthy cause instead of just ten. But this isn't enough for the kind of openness at issue: call it *deep openness*. What's needed is that more than one option was open to you, given everything as it actually was at the time—your mood, all your thoughts and feelings, your brain, your environment, and indeed the entire universe and its entire history. Having been able to have made a different decision if things had been a bit different is one thing; having been able to have made a different decision in the absence of any prior difference is another. The latter requires a kind of flexibility in the brain that I will come back to.

You can think of the these three different views of free will like the standard fuel options at gas stations. Some people opt for premium gas. It's analogous to the soulful, supernatural conception of free will that I described. Others prefer mid-grade gas, which corresponds to the idea of free will that features deep openness and is non-committal about souls. And still others are happy with regular gas, comparable to the remaining view of free will—the one that highlights rationality and the absence of force and is noncommittal about deep openness.

I will not try to evaluate these different ways of concep-tualizing free will here. (If you're interested in a philo-sophical assessment of the matter, you might have a look at my *Free Will and Luck*.) Nor will I try to cajole you into preferring one of them over the others. You should under-stand "free will" as you think best. (But it would make sense to reflect a bit on what "free will" means to you before you take a stand.) If the meaning you assign to "free will" is not outlandish, I predict I will persuade you that science has not closed the door on free will.

Almost everyone who believes in free will—no matter whether they go for premium, mid-grade, or regular free will—believes that the brain plays an indispensable role in generating decisions. (If a soul is involved, it works through the brain somehow.) The challenge that neurosci-ence supposedly poses to free will can't be based simply on the idea that brains are at work in decision making. So what are we supposed to worry about? Here's one answer.

We're supposed to worry that our decisions are produced unconsciously by our brains and that we become aware of them only after the fact. And why is that worrisome? Because it seems that deciding *freely* depends on deciding *consciously*. If all your decisions are made unconsciously, it seems that it's not *up to you* what you decide, and that certainly looks like bad news for free will. Whether anyone has actually proved that all—or even many—of our decisions are made unconsciously is a topic I discuss in Chapters 2 and 3.

Another challenge to the existence of free will that I explore comes from research in social psychology. Some researchers think that our behavior is so powerfully influenced by factors of which we're unaware that there's no room left for free choice—or free will. According to this way of thinking, the various situations in which we find ourselves dictate what we do—in which case, again, what we do isn't up to us.

In this book, I explain why the scientific experiments that are most often claimed to prove that there's no free will in fact leave the existence of free will wide open. I regard this as good news. Here's one reason I do. There's evidence that lowering people's confidence in the existence of free will increases bad behavior. In one study (Vohs and Schooler 2008), people who read passages in which scientists deny that free will exists are more likely to cheat on a subsequent task. In another experiment (Baumeister et al. 2009), college students presented with a series of sentences denying the existence of free will proceeded to behave more aggressively than a control group: they served larger amounts of spicy salsa to people who said they dislike spicy food, despite being told these people had to eat everything on their plates.

Why does this happen? One plausible explanation is pretty straightforward. As your confidence that you have free will diminishes, your impression of yourself as responsible or accountable for what you do weakens. If you're not responsible, you really don't deserve to be blamed for your unseemly actions. And believing that you can't be blamed for acting on your dishonest or aggressive urges reduces your incentive to control them. So you cheat or dish out unpleasantness. We can imagine a student who is piling on the hot salsa thinking, "Hey, you can't blame me for the heartburn you're about to get; I'm not responsible for what I do."

My primary aim is not to spread good news but to set the record straight on what scientists have and have not proved about free will. Of course it's always nice when truth and goodness are on the same side.

I'll lay some of my cards on the table right now and report that I see free will in a positive light. In my view, it exists and belief in it promotes human welfare. Some people who agree with me about the existence of free will put a negative spin on the topic: because free will exists, extremely harsh punishment of criminals is called for, they argue. For the record, justifying punishment has never played any role at all in my writing about free will. My primary concern is to get at the truth about a deep and important issue. But I also worry about the effect of news that there is no free will on unsuspecting readers. Because I worry about that, I have some independent motivation to expose errors in that news. If I were to remain silent about those errors, I would blame myself for not speaking out. When Mark Twain spotted a newspaper account of his death, he drolly announced the truth: "The report of my death was greatly exaggerated." Reports of the death of free will are in the same boat.

In philosophical thought, free will is closely associated with moral responsibility. When the topic is responsibility, people who have much to answer for come quickly to mind. They range from secretive schemers like Bernie Madoff to mass murderers like Adolf Hitler. This pulls one to the dark side of things, but I will steer toward the light. If you see yourself as morally responsible for your future actions, you'll view yourself as having abilities and capacities on which responsibility depends and therefore as having considerable control over what you do—free will, if you like. As

I see it, this outlook is far more accurate than those that portray us as entirely at the mercy of forces beyond our control. What's more, there's evidence that belief in free will promotes personal well-being (Dweck and Molden 2008). There's a lot to be said for free will. I say some of it in what follows.

So how free are we? Let's try to find out.

2 | BENJAMIN LIBET
IF NOT NOW, WHEN?

One person is cited more often than anyone else by scientists who claim that free will is an illusion. Given how influential this scientist's work on free will has been, it's important to understand it, and it's important to see what some of its flaws are and how serious they are. The work at issue was done by neurobiologist Benjamin Libet and began in the early 1980s. It's often said that Libet proved we make all of our decisions unconsciously and therefore never decide anything of our own free will. I'll describe Libet's experimental design and his findings. Then I'll turn to the conclusions he draws and explain why those conclusions aren't justified by the evidence.

Libet's main innovation (1985, 2004) was a method for timing conscious experiences that could then be correlated with measurable brain events. He was particularly interested in experiences of urges, intentions, or decisions.

Participants in the experiments were instructed to flex a wrist whenever they felt like it and then report a bit later on when they first became conscious of their intention or urge to do the flexing.

During the experiment, participants watched a Libet clock. It's fast: a spot revolves around the clock face in about two and a half seconds. The participants, sitting in chairs, reported their belief about where the spot was on the clock when they first became aware of their intention or urge to flex. A bit after they flexed, the clock stopped moving and it was time to make their report. One reporting method was simply to say where participants thought the revolving spot was when they first felt the urge to flex. During my stint as a subject in a Libet-style experiment, I made my reports by moving a cursor to mark that place on a computerized clock.

Readings of electrical conductivity were taken from the scalp, using EEG (electroencephalogram) technology. Brain activity involves measurable electricity—more in some places, depending on what parts of the brain are most active. Think of a telegram, except that brain electricity does the writing.

In order to get readable EEGs, Libet's participants flexed at least forty times during each session. Readings were also taken from the wrist so that Libet could tell when muscle motion began during wrist flexes. At the beginning of muscle motion, there's a surge in muscle activity—a "muscle burst."

There already was evidence from other studies that brain activity increases progressively before individuals make intentional movements. The activity is thought to arise from areas toward the front of the brain that prepare actions and is often measured using EEG. This increased brain activity is called a "readiness potential" or "RP." Libet discovered that when he repeatedly reminded his participants to be spontaneous and not to plan their flexes in advance, he got EEG results that looked like readings for readiness potentials, and they started up about 550 milliseconds—a bit more than half a second—before the muscle started moving (that is, before the muscle burst).

On average, the time of first awareness of the urge, intention, or decision to flex a wrist that participants reported was about 200 milliseconds—one-fifth of a second—before the muscle burst. Libet's take on these results was that the decision to flex right away was made unconsciously about half a second before the wrist muscle moved. That was about a third of a second before the participants became conscious of their decision. Libet believed that in order for free will to be involved in producing bodily actions, the decisions that cause these actions need to be made consciously. So he concluded that free will wasn't playing a role here. And he suggested that we can generalize his findings. That is, Libet suggested that what he thought he found in this particular laboratory setting applies to all of our bodily actions.

Here it is in a nutshell. Libet thought that the decision to *flex now*—not just to flex sooner or later, or at some time or other—was made when the RP began. That was about a half second before muscle motion began. But because people's average time of first reported awareness of the decision was much closer to the time muscle motion begins—about a fifth of a second before it—he concluded that these people became conscious of their decisions to flex only after the decisions had actually been made (see figure 2.1). And because Libet thought that to make a decision freely we need to make it consciously, he concluded that these people did not freely decide to flex and that free will wasn't involved in producing their flexings.

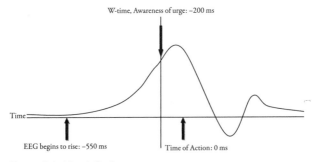

W-time, Awareness of urge: −200 ms

Time

EEG begins to rise: −550 ms

Time of Action: 0 ms

Figure 2.1 Libet's findings.

He also went much further, suggesting that we never make decisions consciously and that free will is never involved in producing bodily actions.

There's a wrinkle, however. Libet believed that once we become aware of our decisions or intentions to do something right away, we have about a tenth of a second to veto them; he thought free will might play a role in vetoing. As someone put it, Libet believed that although we don't have free will, we do have free won't.

Do Libet's experiments prove that there's no free will? No—for several reasons. First, why should we think that a decision is made when the EEG rise begins rather than a few hundred milliseconds later? Maybe what's going on in the brain when the rise begins is a process that might—or might not—*lead to* a decision a bit later. Libet's experiments used a signal to tell a computer to make a record of the preceding couple of seconds of electrical activity. The signal Libet used was the muscle burst. So we don't know whether sometimes—even though the person didn't go on to flex—there was brain activity like what was going on in the participants a half second before they flexed. If we want to find out whether brain activity at a certain time is well correlated with an action at a later time, we need to try to find out whether that brain activity sometimes happens and no corresponding action follows it. Call the first time "R," for "rise begins." And call the later time "R+," for

"R plus about a half second." We need to check to see whether, sometimes, there's a rise at R but no flexing near R+.

Libet didn't look for this. Because of his setup, records of electrical activity were made only when there was muscle motion. So what happened in Libet's experiment at time R—or even R and the next few hundred milliseconds—might have signaled a potential step along the way to a decision to flex, a step that sometimes or often doesn't result in a decision and doesn't result in a flexing. Again, for all we know, on some occasions—maybe many—there was a rise at time R and no associated flexing action.

If decisions weren't actually made when the rise began but were, in fact, made later, then they might have been made consciously. What if they weren't made until about 200 milliseconds before the muscle burst? Then they would have coincided with the average consciousness reports the participants gave. I'll return to this possibility later. It's time to discuss another problem.

Recall that Libet generalized from his findings in this unusual setting to all intentional actions. He suggested that what he thought he discovered here applies to all actions. A comment on my own experience as a subject in a Libet-style experiment will help you see the problem with his assumption. At first, I waited for conscious urges to flex to pop up in me so I'd have something to report when it was time to make the *consciousness* report. I waited until I was pretty sure the urges weren't just going to pop up on their own. I wondered what to do, and I hit on a strategy. I decided that I would just say "now" to myself silently, flex my wrist in response to the silently uttered cue, and then, a little later, try to report where the hand was on the Libet clock when I said "now." (In the experiment I took part in, the Libet clock had a revolving hand rather than a revolving spot.)

If you were to ask me why I said "now" when I did, I'd have to say that I don't know. Why might that be? In Libet's experiment, there's no special reason to pick any particular moment to begin flexing. I had no reason to prefer any given moment for saying "now" over any nearby moment. And I was following my instructions, as any good experimental subject would. That is, I was trying to be spontaneous, and I avoided thinking about when to flex—or when to say "now." The experience resembles going to the supermarket with a shopping list that includes a sixteen-ounce jar of Planters Peanuts. When you get to the peanut display, you just pick up one of those jars. Ordinarily, you have no reason to prefer a particular jar to nearby jars of the same kind. If someone were to ask you why you picked up the jar you just now put in your shopping cart rather than any of the other jars on the shelf, you'd be in my situation when I'm asked why I said "now" when I did. "I don't know" would be an honest answer.

Now, maybe you wouldn't say that free will is involved in picking up the jar of nuts; you might think that free will is too important to be involved in trivial tasks. But even if you think it is involved, free will might work very differently in this scenario rather than when weighing pros and cons and having to make a tough decision. You wouldn't want to generalize from Libet's findings to all decisions—including decisions made after a careful weighing of pros and cons. It's a huge leap to the conclusion that *all* decisions are made unconsciously. Maybe, when we consciously reason about what to do before we decide, we are much more likely to make our decisions consciously.

I drew an analogy between picking a moment to begin flexing and picking up a jar of peanuts. What was I thinking? How similar are these activities? Well, imagine an array of moments set out before you. It's analogous to an array of sixteen-ounce jars of Planters Peanuts at your supermarket. And just as you arbitrarily pick up a jar of peanuts in order to get an item on your shopping list, as a participant in Libet's experiment you would arbitrarily pick a moment to begin flexing in order to comply with part of your instructions. There's no need at all for conscious reasoning about which jar or moment to pick. But in real-life situations in which we do reason consciously about what to do, the road to action seems quite different. It often seems a lot less arbitrary.

In Chapter 1, I express a worry some people have about free will this way: "If all your decisions are made unconsciously, it seems that it's not *up to you* what you decide; and that certainly looks like bad news for free will." How do you interpret the first clause of the quoted sentence? You might think it's saying that conscious thinking plays no role in producing any decisions. But such a conclusion can't be demonstrated by Libet's experiment. After all, the task is to flex a wrist *without consciously thinking* about when to do it. If we want to know whether conscious reasoning ever plays a role in producing decisions, we shouldn't restrict our attention to situations in which people are instructed *not* to think about what to do.

Here is another interpretation of the clause in question: we don't become conscious of any of our decisions until after we make them. As I have explained, Libet didn't show that this is true either. But even if it is true, a bit of lag time—a few hundred milliseconds—between when we actually make a decision on the basis of conscious reasoning and when we are conscious of the decision we made is not a cause for worry. Just as it takes some time for the sounds someone is making to travel to our ears and register in our brain and in our consciousness, it might take a little time for our decisions to show up in our consciousness. But it's not as though conscious reasoning was completely uninvolved in the decision-producing loop. The loop might just be a tad shorter than it seems.

It's time to backtrack a bit. I mentioned Libet's idea that once we become conscious of our intentions, we can veto them. He ran an experiment to test this hypothesis, in which he told the participants to prepare to flex at a certain time—for example, when the spot hit the nine o'clock point on the fast clock—but not to follow through, not to actually flex. To get evidence about what goes on in the brain during this process, he took EEG readings. (In the veto study, what triggered the computer to make an EEG record of the preceding brain activity was the spot reaching the designated point on the clock—the nine o'clock point, say. Libet used the time as a trigger.)

Libet averaged EEG data over many trials. He discovered that a rise began about a second before the designated time and then petered out about 150 to 250 milliseconds before that time. Until it petered out, the EEG readings looked a lot like the readings he found when people flexed at a time the experimenter selected in advance for them. Libet took this to be evidence of the participants' power to veto intentions. He said the participants intended to flex at the nine o'clock point and then vetoed that intention. And he said that the segment of the EEG before the EEG petered out signified the presence of that intention.

Can you put your finger on an error in Libet's reasoning? When I lecture about Libet's veto experiment, I invite the audience to participate in a little experiment of my own. I say that I'm going to count from one to three and that members of the audience should prepare to snap their fingers when I get to three, but not actually snap them. "Prepare to do it, but don't do it," I say. After I say "one," I see people who haven't put their fingers together in preparation to snap, and I jokingly chide them for not playing along.

I count: "One…two…*three*!" And no one snaps! Why not? Because no one intended to snap. What they intended to do was to *prepare* to snap their fingers but not to actually follow through and snap them.

What's the point? There are two points, actually. First, if Libet's participants never intended to flex when the spot reached the nine o'clock point, then his veto experiment doesn't prove that we have the power to veto our intentions. And I bet they didn't intend to flex. I bet they took the same approach as the audience in my finger-snapping experiment.

The second point is more important. You'll recall that Libet got EEG readings in his veto experiment that—for a while, at least—looked like EEG readings in another experiment in which participants were instructed to flex at a preset time—say, the nine o'clock point again. So maybe in that other experiment, too, most of the EEG reading for any given subject—or even the whole second-long reading—isn't zeroing in on an intention. By thinking about the finger-snapping and veto experiments, you can see that preparing to flex at the nine o'clock point isn't the same thing as intending to flex at that point. Perhaps the EEG just picks up on preparing to do something, even when the person doesn't intend to do it—or, in fact, intends *not* to do it, as the cooperative people in my audience intended *not* to snap their fingers. Perhaps it picks up on imagining doing something at a particular time or thinking about doing something soon—or any of these things. This coheres with my earlier suggestion that when the rise starts about half a second before the muscle burst in the main experiment, the beginning of the EEG reading—or the first half of it—is correlated with something that precedes an intention rather than with an intention itself.

This problem with Libet's interpretation of his EEG readings becomes even more vivid when we ask how long it takes for an intention to flex a wrist right away to produce a muscle burst. There's evidence that it takes only about 200 milliseconds—not 550 milliseconds, as would have to be true if Libet were right about when these intentions are formed.

The evidence comes from a go-signal reaction time test. In common go-signal experiments, scientists try to figure out how long it takes a person to respond to a signal with a predesignated action. For example, the go-signal might be the sounding of a tone and the predesignated action might be clicking a mouse button. Participants know what they're supposed to do when they hear the tone, and they're ready to do that. There's a warning signal indicating that a go-signal is coming pretty soon. The participants detect the go-signal and then click as soon as they can.

Once they understand the instructions and agree to participate, the participants have a general intention to click the button whenever they hear the tone. That's different from what I call a *proximal* intention to click the button—an intention to click it *now*. The general intention is something they have throughout the experiment. But if they have proximal intentions to click, they have many of them—one for each click. One possibility is that a general intention—or even a more specific one like an intention to click at the next tone—in combination with hearing the tone produces a proximal intention to click that in turn produces a clicking action. There would be a little causal chain in which a combination of things leads to a proximal intention to click the button, which in turn leads to a clicking action.

If that's how it works, you can get a pretty good idea of how long it takes for a proximal intention to generate a muscle burst. You can time the muscle burst, just as Libet did. You'd know when the tone sounded, as long as you kept track. And since the proximal intention is a response to the tone, it would arise a bit later than the tone. A participant's detecting the tone will take a little time. And if detecting the tone is part of what causes the proximal intention, that will take a little time too.

Libet's participants were watching a fast clock. A go-signal reaction time study in which participants were also watching a Libet clock would give us a helpful comparison. In an experiment of exactly this kind (Haggard and Magno 1999), the mean time between the go-signal and the muscle burst was 231 milliseconds. That's another indication that Libet was wrong in claiming that the proximal intention arises around 550 milliseconds before the muscle burst. It's evidence that the time from proximal intention to muscle burst actually is less than 231 milliseconds. So it's another indication that what happens in the brain about half a second before the muscle moves in Libet's experiment is at most a step along the way to a proximal decision to flex a wrist.

Why does this matter? Because the challenge to free will that Libet's work is supposed to pose rests on his claim that we make all our decisions unconsciously, and that claim is based in significant part on his contention that decisions to flex in his experiments were made about half a second before the muscle burst. This contention about when decisions were made (and so about when proximal intentions to flex appeared on the scene), as I have been explaining, is highly questionable and contrary to our best evidence.

Let's be sure we haven't left any loose ends before we move on. What if go-signals don't cause actions by causing proximal intentions? What if something like an intention to click when the tone next sounds together with the sound of the tone produces a clicking action without producing a proximal intention to click?

That does seem like a possibility. But it should make you wonder whether proximal intentions were at work in Libet's experiment. Here's a parallel idea. In my stint as a subject in a Libet-style experiment, I had a general intention to flex whenever I said "now." And my saying "now" seems like a go-signal. So maybe I didn't have proximal intentions to flex. Maybe my general intention together with my saying "now" produced a flexing action without producing a proximal intention to flex. And maybe something similar is true of other participants in Libet-style experiments. Perhaps some of them use something else as a go-signal—for example, the feeling of an urge. If a general intention plus a go-signal can generate an action without working through a proximal intention, then this very point applies to any participants in Libet's experiment who used some mental event—silently saying "now," feeling an urge to flex, or something else—as a go-signal.

If it turns out that Libet's participants were using an urge as a go-signal and didn't actually have proximal intentions to flex, then their brains were not producing unconscious proximal intentions. Proximal intentions weren't involved. On the other hand, if proximal intentions were involved, the go-signal information suggests they popped up much closer to the time of the muscle burst than Libet believed—maybe around 200 milliseconds before the muscle burst, the average time participants later picked out as the point when they first became aware of their urge.

You will have noticed that I use words like *maybe* and *perhaps* quite a bit in discussing Libet's experiments. That is deliberate. Normally, when I use such words, I am pointing out alternatives to an assumption Libet makes or a conclusion he draws. And I argue that some important alternatives are better supported by the evidence than are Libet's own claims—for example, his claim that decisions were made about half a second before the muscle burst.

It's time for a recap. I begin by summarizing the argument Libet is making.

Libet's argument in a nutshell

1. The participants in Libet's experiments don't make conscious decisions to flex. (Instead, they make their

decisions unconsciously about half a second before the muscle burst and become conscious of them about a third of a second later).

2. So people probably never make conscious decisions to do things.
3. An action is a free action only if it flows from a consciously made decision to perform it.
4. Conclusion: there are probably no free actions.

Here, we have three premises and the conclusion they are meant to support. As I have explained, all three premises are unwarranted. First, there is no good reason to believe that a decision is made about a half second before the muscle burst. The evidence suggests that it is much more likely that any proximal decision to flex is made significantly later. Second, the generalization made in premise 2 is unwarranted. Even if decisions are made unconsciously in a scenario in which there are no pros and cons to assess and nothing to reason about, conscious reasoning about what to do in scenarios in which such reasoning is called for may well increase the probability of conscious decision making. Third, the philosophical claim made in premise 3 is questionable. If informed conscious reasoning leads to a decision that is then put into action, why should it matter if there is a bit of a lag—a couple hundred milliseconds—between when the decision is made and when a person becomes conscious of it? Of course, given that Libet didn't show that the participants in his experiments made unconscious decisions to flex, we don't need to worry much about premise 3. Finally, in light of the problems with the three premises, we can safely conclude that the conclusion of Libet's argument rests on very shaky ground. Libet's experiments come nowhere close to proving that we never act of our own free will.

3 | IS FREE WILL ADRIFT IN NEW-WAVE NEUROSCIENCE?

L ibet's early experiments were conducted over thirty years ago. Because we have more advanced technology now, you may be wondering whether there are recent experiments by neuroscientists that succeed in proving what Libet failed to prove. Two recent neuroscience experiments have been touted in the popular press as devastating challenges to the existence of free will. I'll describe these experiments and explain why the threats they supposedly pose to free will are illusions.

According to a 2008 article by science writer Elsa Youngsteadt, "Researchers have found patterns of brain activity that predict people's decisions up to 10 seconds before they're aware they've made a choice.... The result was hard for some to stomach because it suggested that the unconscious brain calls the shots, making free will an illusory afterthought." Here, as with Libet's work, the idea that our decisions are made unconsciously is at the forefront of a challenge to free will.

The experiment Youngsteadt is writing about (Soon et al. 2008) uses functional magnetic resonance imaging (fMRI) to measure brain activity. This technique measures changes in blood flow in the brain to determine what parts of the brain are most active in a given time period. The study's participants were asked to make many simple decisions while their brain activity was measured using fMRI. Their options were always to press one or the other of two buttons. Nothing hinged on which one they pressed—no reward, no penalty, nothing at all. The scientists say they found that "two brain regions encoded with high accuracy whether the subject was about to choose the left or right response prior to the conscious decision" (p. 544). They report that the "neural information. . . preceded the conscious motor decision by up to" ten seconds.

One point to make right away is that the encoding accuracy in this study actually is only about 60 percent—50 percent being the measure of pure chance, of course. Simply by flipping a coin and basing my prediction on whether it comes up heads or tails—heads for the button on the right and tails for the button on the left—I can predict with 50 percent accuracy which button a participant will press next. And if the person agrees not to press a button for a minute (or an hour), I can make my predictions a minute (or an hour) in advance. I come out ten points worse in accuracy, but I win big on the matter of time.

What are the scientists measuring or detecting several seconds before a button press? What is that neural activity associated with? My bet is a slight unconscious bias toward a particular button on the next press. Possibly, the bias gives the participant about a 60 percent chance of pressing that button next.

By speaking of a bias, all I mean is that the person is slightly more inclined to press one button than the other next time. I'm not saying that the person feels such an inclination or is even aware of it. Put yourself in a participant's shoes. You press one button or the other. You do this many times while trying not to fall into any particular pattern. So you're keeping track, perhaps only in a vague way, of your past button presses. And all this activity may give you a bit more of an inclination to go one way rather than the other next time—an inclination you may or may not be aware of. I'll return to this idea shortly.

These participants are like the shopper in my peanuts example. The shopper doesn't care about getting a particular jar, as long as it's a sixteen-ounce jar of Planters Peanuts. They're also like the participants in Libet's experiment—except that they're picking a button to press for no particular reason instead of picking a moment to begin pressing for no particular reason. Maybe this kind of picking doesn't have much to do with free will. But even if it does, it would be difficult to generalize from findings in this sphere to claims about what happens when people have to make hard choices and are consciously reasoning about what to.

An old fable is relevant here—the fable of Buridan's ass. Because this ass was hyper-rational, it would never do a thing unless it had a better reason to do it than anything else. One day, this special donkey was hungry and found itself midway between two equally large and equally attractive bales of hay. It looked to the left and looked to the right. It had no reason to prefer either bale over the other. So it just stood there and eventually starved to death. Poor ass!

In the fMRI experiment I'm discussing, as in Libet's experiments, the participants are in a situation like the ass's. The solution is just to pick. If the ass had arbitrarily picked a bale of hay, its story would have had a happy ending. The participants in the fMRI study did arbitrarily pick a button to press—sometimes the one on the left, and sometimes the one on the right. My concern now is that this kind of picking may not be very similar to choosing or deciding in situations in which a lot of conscious weighing of reasons—pros and cons—goes into the choice or decision. How similar is the arbitrary picking of a button to a decision to ask one's spouse for a divorce—or to change careers or start a small business—after protracted reflection on reasons for and against that decision? If arbitrary picking is not very similar to these other decisions, claiming that what happens in instances of arbitrary picking also happens in instances of complicated, painstaking decision making is a huge stretch.

Another problem is that a 60-percent accuracy rate in predicting which button a participant will press next doesn't seem to be much of a threat to free will. As I explained, the prediction—made several seconds in advance of a press—might be based on brain activity that reflects a slight bias toward picking one button on the next go. But slight biases certainly don't seem to rule out free will. They don't dictate or compel behavior. They're nothing more than nudges.

Next on our agenda is a recent experiment using depth electrodes (Fried et al. 2011). Although depth electrodes have been used since the 1950s, the technology is more sophisticated now. People with severe epilepsy sometimes opt for a procedure that requires removing part of the skull. Electrodes are placed on the surface of the brain— and sometimes a bit beneath the surface. The purpose is to identify places where seizures are generated so surgery can be performed on the areas of the brain responsible for the seizures. Electrical recordings directly from the brain are much more informative than EEG readings, since the electricity measured by EEG has to travel through the thick bone of the skull.

If patients wished, they could participate in various brain studies, including Libet-style studies, while the electrodes were in place. In one such study, Fried and colleagues were able to predict something with 80 percent accuracy. The participants were asked to press a key whenever they wanted and then make a report after they pressed it. They reported their belief about where the hand was on a Libet clock when they first felt the urge to press the key. This is a belief about what the experimenters call "W time" (a term borrowed from Libet). With readings taken directly from neurons in the supplementary motor area of the brain, the experimenters were able to predict what time participants would report. They were able to do this 700 milliseconds—seven-tenths of a second—before W time. Actually, I should be a bit more precise: 80 percent of the time, significant changes in neural activity were detected about 700 milliseconds before the W time the participant later reported, and the W time the scientists predicted was within a few hundred milliseconds of the W time the participant reported.

As the experimenters realize, the timing task is tricky. Just think about it. Participants are looking into their minds for an urge and trying to match an urge's popping up in consciousness with their perception of a clock hand that is moving very fast. But let's not get sidetracked by that.

The punch line is that pretty specific brain activity seems to lead to conscious urges to press the key. I mentioned that the recordings were done from the supplementary motor area, an area involved in the preparation and production of bodily actions.

How is this supposed to challenge free will? The scientists who conducted this experiment don't make claims about free will in the article I'm discussing. But others see the results as threatening free will. They propose that unconscious brain activity has already determined when the participants will press the key, even before they become aware of their conscious urge to press it.

But has it? Two points should be made. First, given that the predictions are correct only 80 percent of the time, there's no particular reason to believe that determinism is involved. Second, even if urges to press are determined by unconscious brain activity, it may be up to the participants whether they act on those urges or not. Libet said that some of the participants in his experiments reported that they occasionally vetoed urges to flex. They said they then waited for another urge to come along before flexing. This suggests that even if an *urge* is determined by unconscious brain processes, those processes might not determine a corresponding action. By the way, if you were a participant in Libet's study, flexing spontaneously at least forty times, you might deal with the tedium by seeing what it felt like to veto an urge every once in a while.

I had been wondering how long I could carry on without using the word *determinism*. You'll notice that it shows up in the previous paragraph. What is determinism then? In mainstream philosophical writing about free will, as in physics, determinism is the idea that a complete description of the universe at any time—fifty years ago, shortly after the Big Bang, or whenever—together with a complete list of all the laws of nature entails everything that's true about the universe, including everything that will ever happen. One statement entails another when, *necessarily*, if the first statement is true, then so is the second. We ask, "Does statement A entail statement B?" If there's no possible way for the first statement to be true without the second one being true, then the answer is yes. So let statement A be a complete description of the universe a billion years ago together with a complete list of all the laws of nature, and let statement B be that I ate cornflakes for breakfast today (which is true). If determinism is true of our universe, then there's no possible way for statement A to be true without it also being true that I ate cornflakes for breakfast today. If determinism is *not* true of our universe, statement A is compatible both with my eating cornflakes for breakfast today and with my doing something else instead.

You've heard the expression "free will versus determinism." Some people who use it don't mean much more by *determinism* than "something or other that is incompatible with free will." But I'm not using it in that sense. And by the way, determinism as I have described it isn't a force. It's just a way a universe is if a statement about it like A entails all the other true statements about it.

Just yesterday, a reporter from a local newspaper phoned me. He said he'd heard about my Big Questions in Free Will project and thought I might be able to answer a question for him. His question was whether God cares which teams win football games. When I asked how this question is related to free will, he mentioned determinism. And when I asked him what he meant by determinism, he was stumped for a while. Eventually, he described determinism as a force that makes free will impossible. I explained to him, as I explained to you, that philosophers and physicists have something much more definite in mind.

OK, back to neuroscience. A thought experiment proposed by neuroscientist V. S. Ramachandran is interesting in connection with the question about what might or might not be up to the participants in the experiments I've been discussing. Based on Libet's experiment, it starts as follows: "I'm monitoring your EEG while you wiggle your finger.... I will see a readiness potential a second before you act. But suppose I display the signal on a screen in front of you so that you can *see* your free will. Every time you are about to wiggle your finger, supposedly using your own free will, the machine will tell you a second in advance!" (2004, p. 87).

Ramachandran asks what you would experience, and he offers an answer:

> There are three logical possibilities. (1) You might experience a sudden loss of will, feeling that the machine is controlling you, that you are a mere puppet and that free will is just an illusion.. . . (2) You might think that it does not change your sense of free will one iota, preferring to believe that the machine has some sort of spooky paranormal precognition by which it is able to predict your movements accurately. (3) You might ... deny the evidence of your eyes and maintain that your sensation of will preceded the machine's signal.

Did Ramachandran overlook an important logical possibility? If I were a participant in the experiment, I'd definitely want to test the machine's powers. I'd watch for the signal to appear on the screen and then see if I could keep from wiggling a finger. Libet's data definitely leave this possibility open. I might even produce EEG readings that look like the ones found in Libet's veto experiment. The other experiments I've been discussing leave this possibility open too.

Consider the following two sentences:

1. Whenever you wiggle your finger, signal S appears a second before you wiggle it.
2. Whenever signal S appears, you wiggle your finger a second later.

These sentences say two very different things. This is easy to see, especially when you consider two parallel sentences.

3. Whenever you win a lottery prize, you acquired a lottery ticket before you won—for example, you bought it or found it.
4. Whenever you acquire a lottery ticket, you win a lottery prize.

You can't win a lottery unless you first get a ticket, as sentence 3 reports. But that doesn't mean that every ticket is a winner, as sentence 4 falsely asserts. Similarly, maybe you can't wiggle your finger unless signal S first appears; but that doesn't mean that every time the signal appears, you'll wiggle your finger.

If you succeed in keeping your finger still after you see the signal, maybe the signal is a sign of the presence of a potential cause of a proximal intention or decision to wiggle your finger. Even when that potential cause is present, you might decide not to wiggle your finger and you might behave accordingly. In that case, you won't see the machine as controlling you; you won't be tempted to believe the machine has paranormal predictive powers; and you won't deny the evidence of your eyes. In short, you won't do any of the three possible things Ramachandran mentioned. You'll do a fourth possible thing—one he didn't mention.

In the neuroscience experiments I've been discussing, participants are supposed to wait for an urge and then act on it. They're not supposed to plan in advance—or even think about—when to flex or click a key. In the fMRI experiment, too, there's no thinking about what to do: participants just arbitrarily pick a button to press, maybe in response to an urge. So we shouldn't expect the urges to arise out of conscious processes. But, of course, they don't just come out of the blue. That is, they have causes. If the urges don't arise out of conscious processes, they arise out of unconscious ones. But that doesn't mean that unconscious processes dictate behavior. Fortunately, as you know very well from experience, we don't act on all our urges.

Toward the end of Chapter 2, I set out Libet's reasoning as a brief argument with numbered premises and a conclusion. People who believe that the much more recent experiments discussed in this chapter threaten the existence of free will would seem to be reasoning along similar lines, as follows.

New-wave Libet-style Argument in a Nutshell

1. The participants in the fMRI and depth electrode experiments don't make conscious decisions to press buttons or click keys. (Instead, they make their decisions unconsciously well before they become conscious of them.)
2. So probably people never make conscious decisions to do things.
3. An action is a free action only if it flows from a consciously made decision to perform it.
4. Conclusion: probably there are no free actions.

The main problems with Libet's version of the argument apply here as well. First, there is no good reason to believe that the early brain activity the scientists detected is correlated with an early decision. Second, spontaneous picking of a button—or moment—to press is so different from decisions that seem to flow from a careful weighing of pros and cons that it's a mistake to generalize from the alleged findings to all decisions. What happens in scenarios featuring spontaneous picking may be very different from what happens in scenarios in which we spend a lot of time and effort weighing pros and cons before we decide what to do. And, third, the philosophical issues surrounding premise 3 haven't changed; they are just as I describe in Chapter 2.

4 | GOOD INTENTIONS

Some challenges to free will come from neuroscience, and others come from branches of science that are focused more on human behavior than the human brain. It's time to move on to the main behavior-based challenges to free will. They definitely are interesting; and, as you'll see, some are quite disturbing.

Social psychologist Daniel Wegner wrote a book entitled *The Illusion of Conscious Will*. One of its main themes is that conscious intentions are never among the causes of corresponding actions. He regards that as ruling out free will. After all, if our conscious intentions to do things have no effect at all on whether or not we do them, it would seem that what we do isn't up to us. And if what we do is never up to us, it is hard to see how we can ever act freely.

I said "among the causes." That might be unclear, so let me explain what I have in mind. Suppose someone says that her conscious intention to buy this book caused her to buy it. That might suggest that her intention was the only cause of this. But, of course, there were other causes, including causes of her intention. (Her intention didn't come out of the blue; it had causes too.) I assume that causes of her intention are also (less direct) causes of what her intention causes. I say "among the causes" to acknowledge this (and more). I could have said that her conscious intention was *a* cause of her buying the book. As long as you don't read "*a* cause" as "*the* cause," that would work for me.

Wegner uses two kinds of argument for his thesis that free will is an illusion. One kind is based on Libet's work, which I examine in Chapter 2. The other kind of argument appeals to evidence about automatic actions and evidence of certain kinds of mistakes people make about actions.

I'll start with some experiments on automaticity done in the late nineteenth century with an automatograph (see Wegner 2002). Participants placed a hand on the glass plate on top of this device. Even tiny movements of that plate were detected by an attached recording device. A screen prevented the participant from seeing what was being recorded (see figure 4.1).

Suppose you had your hand on the contraption. If I started a metronome and asked you to count its clicks, you might unknowingly make tiny hand movements in

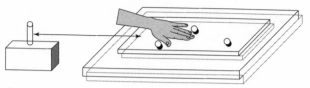

Figure 4.1 Automatograph.

time with the rhythm. If I asked you to think of the nearest street, you might slowly and unconsciously move your hand toward that street. If I got you to hide something in my office and then asked you to think about the object, you might—without realizing it—very slowly move your hand in its direction. If I ask you whether you moved your hand and you say you didn't, we have evidence that people sometimes perform actions that they're not conscious of and don't consciously intend. Evidence of this kind is a plank in Wegner's argument that conscious proximal intentions are never among the causes of corresponding actions.

Wegner offers further evidence. A technique called "facilitated communication" was intended to help people with communication problems caused by such conditions as severe autism or cerebral palsy. Trained facilitators had the job of helping these people touch keys on a keyboard—keys the clients were trying to touch in order to type sentences. Facilitators were supposed to avoid controlling their clients' movements. They were there just to help out. Many intended to do precisely this—and they believed that was all they were doing. It was discovered, however, that these facilitators were actually unknowingly controlling what keys were being pressed and therefore what was being typed. In fact, sometimes the information typed out was known to the facilitator but not to the client. The facilitators were the real authors of the sentences typed out on the keyboard. This is another example of people performing actions unknowingly and without consciously intending to perform them.

Wegner also discusses a spiritualist phenomenon called "table turning" that was popular in the nineteenth century. People would join together and put their hands on a table, hoping that spirits would move it. Sometimes, the table would move. The people were moving it, of course—apparently without realizing they were, and without consciously intending to move it.

Wegner's book describes a phenomenon in the clinical sphere. A certain kind of damage to the frontal lobes causes something called "utilization behavior." If you have the disorder and someone touches your hands with an empty glass and a pitcher of water, you might automatically fill the glass with water. If I touch your hand with eyeglasses, you might put them on. And if I try the same thing with another pair of glasses, you might put them on right over the glasses you're wearing. Wegner suggests that the route to action in such cases bypasses intention—that what happens is a kind of automatic response to a stimulus. That's similar to what happens in the experiments with the automatograph. There the stimuli are the clicks of the metronome and being asked to think about the nearest street or the object you hid.

How does Wegner move from evidence like this to the conclusion that conscious intentions are *never* among the causes of corresponding actions? He takes an all-or-nothing stand.

> It has to be one way or the other. Either the automatisms are oddities against the general backdrop of conscious behavior causation in everyday life, or we must turn everything around quite radically and begin to think that behavior that occurs *with* a sense of will is somehow the odd case, an add-on to a more basic underlying system. (2002, p. 144)

If it has to be one way or the other, then all actions have to be caused in the same basic way. So if *some* actions are produced by automatic mechanisms rather than by conscious intentions, then *all* of them are.

I'm willing to grant that the hand movements on the automatograph, the controlling actions by the facilitators, and various other actions aren't caused by conscious intentions to perform them. But I'm unwilling to accept that all actions are caused in basically the same way. I'll come back to this after I discuss evidence that conscious intentions sometimes *are* among the causes of corresponding actions.

There's an important body of research on implementation intentions—intentions to do a thing at a certain place and time or in a certain situation. I'll give you some examples. In one experiment, the participants were women who wanted to do a breast self-examination during the next month. The women were divided into two groups. There was only one difference in what they were instructed to do. One group was asked to decide during the experiment on a place and time to do the examination the next month, and the other group wasn't. The first group wrote down what they decided before the experiment ended and turned the note in. Obviously, they were conscious of what they were writing down. They had *conscious* implementation intentions.

The results were impressive. All of the women given the implementation intention instruction did complete a breast exam the next month, and all but one of them did it at basically the time and place they decided on in advance. But only 53 percent of the women from the other group performed a breast exam the following month.

In another experiment, participants were informed of the benefits of vigorous exercise. Again, there were two groups. One group was asked to decide during the experiment on a place and time for twenty minutes of exercise the next week, and the other group wasn't given this instruction. The vast majority—91 percent—of those in the implementation intention group exercised the following week, compared to only 39 percent of the other group.

In a third experiment, the participants were recovering drug addicts who would be looking for jobs soon. All of them were supposed to write resumes by the end of the day. One group was asked in the morning to decide on a place and time later that day to carry out that task. The other group was asked to decide on a place and time to eat lunch. None of the people in the second group wrote a resume by the end of the day, but 80 percent of the first group did.

I've only given you three examples. (All three are reviewed by Peter Gollwitzer in a very useful 1999 article.) A 2006 review article by Peter Gollwitzer and Paschal Sheeran reports that ninety-four independent tests of implementation intentions showed that they had a significant effect on behavior. The number is much higher now.

Consciously formulating implementation intentions to do things makes people more likely to do them. Take the breast exam experiment, for example. All women in the control group had some motivation to do the breast exam, and many of them may have intended at the time to do one the next month, but without consciously deciding in advance on a place and time. Yet, only 53 percent of these women performed the self-exam, whereas all the women given the implementation intention instruction did so. In light of this remarkable difference, it's difficult to deny that the implementation intentions did important causal work. But how important is it that they were *conscious* intentions? Would unconscious implementation intentions have worked just as well?

What kind of experiment could be used to test the hypothesis that unconscious implementation intentions work as well as conscious ones? The experimenters would have to find a way to induce unconscious implementation intentions and then see whether they work as well as conscious ones. And how would they know whether they succeeded in inducing unconscious implementation intentions? If they tried to induce them in, say, the breast self-exam situation and found that the women they were studying did significantly better than the control group, that would be evidence that implementation intentions were successfully introduced. And if experimenters asked their participants whether they had any specific plan for a place and time to do a breast exam and the participants said no, that would indicate that the participants weren't conscious of such intentions. Constructing an experiment that yields evidence both that implementation intentions were induced and that the participants weren't conscious of these intentions would be a challenging task indeed. On this issue, my attitude is "I'll believe it when I see it."

In any case, we have a good idea how *conscious* implementation intentions work. Presumably, in the three studies I described, people consciously remember—at the right time—the intention they consciously reported earlier. And the fact that they consciously remember it increases the likelihood that they'll actually act on their intention and perform the breast exam, do the exercise routine, or write the resume. The conscious remembering would certainly help me. Forgetting what I intended to do is a problem I have occasionally.

Someone might insist that the neural correlates of the conscious implementation intentions rather than the conscious intentions themselves do the real causal work. The idea isn't that unconscious intentions are doing the work. Rather, it's that neurochemical events associated with conscious implementation intentions are.

The issue here is metaphysical, a problem for those who specialize in dealing with deep philosophical questions about the nature of reality rather than for scientists. At an inopportune moment, you might embarrass yourself by saying something that strikes you as so stupid that you blush. Someone might say that it's not your hearing yourself but the neural correlate of that auditory event that caused the embarrassment and the blushing. This person might also say that your embarrassment itself isn't a cause of the blushing and that, in fact, the neural correlate of your embarrassment causes the blushing. That's a metaphysical issue. If scientists can't separate a feeling of embarrassment from its neural correlate and see what happens when each one is present without the other one, they can't test to see which of them is doing the causal work.

It's time for a recap. One of Wegner's ideas is that having free will depends on your conscious intentions sometimes being among the causes of corresponding actions. And another of his ideas is that conscious intentions never actually cause actions; instead, unconscious mechanisms do. The second idea has two main parts. First, there is evidence that some of our actions aren't caused by conscious intentions. Second, all actions are caused in basically the same way. Putting those two parts together produces the conclusion that conscious intentions are never among the causes of corresponding actions.

The argument can be represented as follows.

Wegner's automaticity argument in a nutshell

1. Some human actions aren't caused even partly by conscious intentions (and the same goes for the neural

correlates of conscious intentions; some actions aren't caused by them either).

2. All human actions are caused in basically the same way.

3. So no human actions are caused even partly by conscious intentions (and the same goes for the neural correlates of conscious intentions). (from 1 and 2)

4. People don't have free will unless their conscious intentions (or their neural correlates) are sometimes among the causes of corresponding actions.

5. So people don't have free will. (from 3 and 4)

This argument is unpersuasive. First, why do all actions have to be caused in the same way? There's a big difference between unknowingly moving my hand in the direction of an object I hid or toward the street I'm thinking about and intentionally leaving my hotel room by 8:00 a.m. in order to show up on time for an important meeting in a city I'm visiting for the first time. For one thing, although my hand movements involved no conscious planning, my decision about when to leave was preceded by conscious information gathering about the best route to the meeting and how long it would take to get there. Second, I described evidence that conscious intentions sometimes are effective, that is, evidence that they lead to the intended actions. If conscious intentions (or their neural correlates) are sometimes among the causes of corresponding actions, then Wegner's threat to free will disappears.

Wegner says that something he regards as *necessary* for free will never happens. And I'm saying that this necessary thing sometimes does happen—that conscious intentions (or their neural correlates) sometimes are among the causes of corresponding actions. Wegner's claim that conscious intentions are *never* among the causes of human actions is a very bold one. It's about every single action that any human being has ever performed. Yet, he backs it up only with Libet's data and evidence from fringe cases, combined with the highly disputable assertion that all human actions are caused in basically the same way (if the fringe actions and wrist flexes in Libet's experiments don't have conscious intentions among their causes, then no human actions do). My claim that conscious intentions (or their neural correlates) are among the causes of *some* human actions is much less bold. And I have backed it up with directly relevant, powerful evidence about conscious implementation intentions. Think about it: which of us is on firmer ground here?

5 | TOUGH SITUATIONS

"When we set out to explain our actions," neuroscientist Michael Gazzaniga writes, "they are all post hoc explanations, using post hoc observations with no access to nonconscious processing" (2011, p. 77). This remark, in a book entitled *Who's in Charge? Free Will and the Science of the Brain*, bridges neuroscience experiments of the kind I discuss in earlier chapters to the social psychology experiments I explore in this chapter. What's the connection to free will? Well, if we never know why we're going to do what we're about to do, then it would seem that it's never actually up to us what we do. And if what we do is never up to us, we never act freely. That seems pretty straightforward. But is Gazzaniga right?

I read Gazzaniga's book on a flight to a conference in Munich. People who invite philosophy professors to conferences rarely are willing to spring for a seat in first class, and this occasion was no exception. I like extra legroom on planes. So right after I buy a coach ticket online, I check the airline website for an exit row seat—first on the aisle and then next to a window. If I find a seat I like, I snatch it up. I do all this consciously. (I don't know how to look for exit row seats unconsciously, even if computer programs can do it.) And I do it because I have a conscious preference for extra legroom on long flights and know—consciously—how to get the extra room for my legs without paying more than my hosts are willing to spend. If someone had asked me to explain why I chose the seat I chose, I could have offered a fine explanation partly in terms of a conscious preference I had when I was going about the business of selecting a seat. My explanation would have been based on some facts about what I wanted and was thinking before I selected the seat and while I selected it—not on observations I made *after* I selected it.

Why does Gazzaniga sell our mental life short? Partly because he is overly impressed by some of the experiments he discusses—well-known experiments by Benjamin Libet and more recent work by Chun Siong Soon and colleagues, which you'll remember from earlier chapters.

You'll recall that on the basis of brain activity as measured by blood flow, Soon and colleagues were able to predict with 60 percent accuracy, about ten seconds in advance, whether a person would press the button on the left or the button on the right. People were supposed to decide on a button and then press it. They all did this many times, knowing that nothing hinged on which button they pressed.

What does the early brain activity at issue signify? Perhaps just an unconscious bias toward a particular button, as I explained. In any case, there is no reason to prefer either button over the other. So if the person were asked why he pressed the left button this time, he should say something like: "I just randomly picked it, because I'm following your instructions." Because there is no place in the experiment for conscious reflection about which button to press, there is no place for an explanation of the button pressing in terms of conscious reasons for pressing it. The same general point applies to Libet's studies; his subjects arbitrarily pick a moment to begin flexing a wrist.

When I select an exit row seat, things are very different. I know I have a reason—a good one—to select such a seat rather than an ordinary seat in coach. And because I do, I consciously look online for an available seat in an exit row. By the way, given what I have told you, you can predict with close to 100 percent accuracy what I will try to do next time I buy a coach seat on a long flight. And you have achieved this degree of accuracy simply by consciously attending to what I wrote.

I described Gazzaniga's remark about post hoc explanations as a bridge from neuroscience experiments that I've discussed to social psychology experiments that also merit serious attention. It's time to see what's on the other side of the bridge.

I'm about to tackle some experiments that are regarded as providing powerful evidence that human behavior is strongly influenced by things other than conscious reasons. Gazzaniga is getting at that from another angle. Whether the influence of these other things makes it true that free will is an illusion is a question I will explore. First, I need to describe some of the experiments. I've decided to focus on three classic studies.

A famous experiment on the behavior of bystanders was inspired by an electrifying episode in New York City in 1964. According to newspaper reports, although many people witnessed the early morning stabbing of Kitty Genovese from their apartment windows, no one tried to stop the assault, and no one even called the police.

In a study conducted by John Darley and Bibb Latané (1968) in the wake of the Genovese murder, participants were told that they would be talking about personal problems associated with being a college student. Each was in a room alone, thinking that he or she was talking to other participants over a microphone. Participants were led to believe that there was only one other participant (group

A), that there were two others (group B), or that there were five others (group C). In fact, the voices the participants heard were recordings. Participants were told that while one person was talking, the microphone arrangement would not let anyone else talk. At some point, the participant would hear a person—the "victim"—say that he felt like he was about to have a seizure. The victim would ask for help, ramble a bit, say that he was afraid he might die, and so on. His voice would be abruptly cut off after he talked for 125 seconds, just after he made choking sounds.

The percentage figures for participants who left the cubicle to help before the voice was cut off are as follows: group A, 85 percent; group B, 62 percent; and group C, 31 percent. Also, all the participants in group A eventually reported the emergency, whereas only 62 percent of the participants in group C did this. Clearly, participants' beliefs about how many other people could hear the voice—none, one, or four—had an effect on their behavior. Even so, there being one or four other people around to help the victim seems, in itself, no reason not to help.

Preparations for the next study, Philip Zimbardo's Stanford prison experiment (Haney et al. 1973), began with newspaper ads seeking male college students willing to take part in an experiment on prison life. The volunteers selected as prisoners were arrested at their residences, handcuffed, searched, and driven in a police car to a Palo Alto police station. After being fingerprinted and placed in a detention cell, they were driven to the mock prison built in the basement of the Stanford psychology building. When they arrived, they were stripped and sprayed with deodorant. Then, after being given a prison uniform and photographed, they were locked in cells. There were three small cells—six feet by nine feet—for the ten prisoners and a very small solitary confinement cell. There were also rooms for volunteers selected as guards. Much of the activity was videoed by hidden cameras. Concealed microphones picked up conversations.

The experiment was to run for two weeks. The prisoners were there twenty-four hours a day. The guards worked eight-hour shifts and then went home. Prisoners had three simple, bland meals a day and the same number of supervised toilet visits. They were also lined up three times each day to be counted and were always referred to by a number worn on their uniform—never by their name. They had two hours of free time each day to write letters or read, unless that privilege was taken away. And they had chores to do—cleaning toilets and the like. It's interesting to note that during their free time, 90 percent of what the prisoners talked about had to do with their prison life.

Zimbardo and coauthors report that "five prisoners…had to be released because of extreme emotional depression, crying, rage and acute anxiety" (Haney et al. 1973, p. 81). Although the experiment was supposed to last two weeks, Zimbardo ended it after just six days. One prisoner had to be released after thirty-six hours owing to "extreme depression, disorganized thinking, uncontrollable crying and fits of rage" (Zimbardo et al. 1973). Another developed a psychosomatic rash.

Several of the guards became bullies, and those who didn't participate in the bullying allowed it to continue. The harassment increased each day. Counting the prisoners initially took ten minutes, but later went on for hours. During these counts, prisoners were encouraged to belittle each other. Over time, the prisoners' attitudes toward one another reflected the guards' attitudes toward them. Insults and threats escalated, and so did commands to do pointless or demeaning tasks. Guards sometimes made prisoners clean toilets with their bare hands.

Pointless tasks included moving boxes back and forth from one closet to another and picking thorns out of blankets after guards had dragged the blankets through bushes. Sometimes prisoners would be made to do push-ups while guards stepped on them. Guards would wake prisoners up in the middle of the night to count them. Sometimes guards denied prisoners their scheduled leisure time just for the fun of it or locked them in a solitary confinement cell for no good reason. The "cell" was a seven-foot-tall broom closet two feet wide and two feet deep. After the 10:00 p.m. lockup, prisoners often had to use buckets in their cells as toilets. On the second day of the experiment, prisoners staged a protest. The guards used a fire extinguisher to spray them, stripped them, and put the protest leaders in solitary confinement.

The guards created a "privilege" cell to sow dissension among the prisoners. The good prisoners would use the cell and get better treatment, including better food. To confuse the prisoners, guards later gave this privilege to the prisoners who seemed worse. Some of the guards even became sadistic. Of course, Zimbardo was as interested in the effects on the guards as the effects on the prisoners.

Bad effects of the situation showed up both in prisoners and in guards. The guards fell into three types. Some were tough but fair, some were good guys who did small favors for prisoners, and about a third were hostile and abusive. None of the testing the experimenters did in advance predicted which of the students would become power-loving guards. Some of the guards were disappointed that the experiment ended early; they enjoyed their power.

One of the prisoners felt sick and wanted to be released. He cried hysterically while talking with Zimbardo (in his role as prison superintendent) and a priest. After Zimbardo left the room to get the prisoner some food, the other prisoners began to chant that this one was a bad prisoner. When Zimbardo realized that the prisoner could hear this, he ran back into the room. He writes:

> I suggested we leave, but he refused. Through his tears, he said he could not leave because the others had labeled him a bad prisoner. Even though he was feeling sick, he wanted to go back and prove he was not a bad prisoner. At that point I said, "Listen, you are not #819. You are [his name], and my name is Dr. Zimbardo. I am a psychologist, not a prison superintendent, and this is not a real prison. This is just an experiment, and those are students, not prisoners, just like you. Let's go." He stopped crying suddenly, looked up at me like a small child awakened from a nightmare, and replied, "Okay, let's go." (Zimbardo n.d.)

This episode with the unfortunate young man makes especially salient how deeply participants were drawn into their roles.

I turn to psychologist Stanley Milgram's famous studies of obedience, beginning with his 1963 report. Milgram wanted to understand why people obey commands to do horrible things they wouldn't do on their own. Many Nazi soldiers who worked in prison camps might be cases in point.

Forty men between the ages of twenty and fifty and from many walks of life participated in the experiment. They were told that they would take part in an experiment about how punishment is related to memory. At the beginning, each participant met the experimenter (actually, a high school teacher playing the role of an experimenter) and a confederate of his. The participant was told that he and the other man would draw slips of paper from a hat to see which of them would be the "teacher" and which the "learner." In fact, the participant was always the teacher. He heard the cover story and saw an electrified chair in which the learner would sit during the experiment. While sitting in the wired chair, the learner supposedly would receive an electric shock from the teacher each time he gave an incorrect answer. The teacher watched the learner being strapped into the electric chair and was told that the straps would prevent him from moving too much while being shocked. The teacher then moved to another room where he could no longer see the learner. Milgram reported that, with a few exceptions, participants believed the setup was real. (It wasn't, of course. There were no actual shocks.)

Participants were shown an array of thirty levers, each associated with different degrees of shock. The lowest shock was for the first incorrect answer, the second lowest was for the second wrong answer, and so on. Sets of levers—mainly sets of four—were labeled. About half way through the sequence of severity, the label read "intense shock," followed by "extreme intensity shock," "danger: severe shock," and finally "XXX."

The learner answered by pressing a button. At one point during the experiment—after he had received his twentieth shock—the learner pounded on the wall, and from then on he did not answer any more questions. The twentieth shock was delivered by the fourth lever in the "intense shock" level. The shock levels were also labeled with voltage numbers. That lever was labeled "300 volts." Before shocking the learner, the teacher had to report the voltage of the shock he was about to administer, ranging from 15 volts at the beginning all the way up to 450 volts at the end. At the beginning of the experiment, the scientist told the teacher that "although the shocks can be extremely painful, they cause no permanent tissue damage." When participants raised the issue of stopping the experiment, they were given stock replies ranging from "Please continue" to "You have no other choice, you *must* go on." The scientist started with a simple request to continue and eventually moved up to the "no choice" response if the participant persisted in talking about stopping.

Twenty-six of the forty participants continued to apply shocks to the learners all the way to the end. (Teachers were told that the absence of an answer counted as a wrong answer.) No participant stopped administering shocks before the twentieth shock. Five stopped right after that one. Four stopped after the next one: it was the first shock in the series labeled "extreme intensity shock" and the first shock in response to a non-answer. The other four dropped out a bit later.

Milgram reports that the teachers displayed enormous tension, fits of nervous laughter, twitching, stuttering, sweating, and the like. And when they talked about stopping, a calm reply by the experimenter often worked: "The experiment requires that you continue," "It is absolutely essential that you continue," or the like. If a participant refused to continue after being told he had no choice, the experiment was terminated and the participant was debriefed. This "no choice" response was the last in a series of four stock responses by the experimenter.

Milgram conducted many versions of this experiment. Brief descriptions of three additional versions will prove useful. In "Voice-Feedback" (Milgram 1974, experiment 2), the teacher could now hear the learner speak. The learner grunts in response to the 75-volt shock and the slightly later ones. At 120 volts—labeled "moderate"—he shouts and says the shocks are becoming painful. He groans after the next shock, and he refuses to continue in response to the one after that—the tenth shock. This goes on with increasing intensity for several more shocks. At

180 volts, the learner screams that he cannot stand the pain. By 270 volts he is screaming in agony. At 300 volts—the twentieth shock—he desperately shouts that he will not provide any more answers. And he repeats this after the next shock—after emitting a violent scream. After all subsequent shocks, he shrieks in agony. Twenty-five of the forty participants administered shocks all the way to the end. And in a version of the experiment in which the learner refers to his heart condition at 150, 195, and 330 volts, the results are about the same. Twenty-six of the forty teachers went all the way.

In two other versions of the experiment, the teacher was brought much closer to the learner, but everything else was very similar—the groaning, screaming, and so on. In one version ("Proximity," Milgram 1974, experiment 3), the teacher was just a foot and a half from the learner and could see him clearly. In the other ("Touch-Proximity," Milgram 1974, experiment 4), the learner could remove his hand from a shock plate in order to avoid being shocked, and the teacher would have to force the learner's hand onto the plate in order to shock him. In "Proximity," sixteen of the forty participants continued to the end. In "Proximity-Touch," twelve of the forty did.

The situationist findings I've described (along with findings of many related studies) certainly are interesting. What should we make of them? According to a pessimistic view, we have very little control over our behavior—human behavior is largely driven by the situations in which we find ourselves and the effects these situations have on unconscious, automatic behavior-producing processes. As the pessimist sees things, conscious reflection plays no role in guiding our actions.

I'm not so pessimistic. I'll explain why, beginning with an anecdote.

A few days after the tragic events of September 11, 2001, a friend said, "That will never happen again." He explained that, in his view, people would learn from what happened, and henceforth, a plane full of passengers would not go down without a fight. They would resist, and they would overpower their foes. That was an uplifting thought (inspired partly by news reports that passengers and crew on United Airlines flight 93 had heard about the earlier crashes and attempted to regain control of their own doomed plane).

The role of "passenger" on a commercial flight is pretty well defined. Passengers are to sit down, fasten their seat belts, keep them fastened until they are permitted to get up, refrain from being disruptive in any way, and, in general, obey the airline employees. For the most part, if there is a disturbance, passengers expect that the flight crew will deal with it. The passengers' situation involves ingredients of the three studies I described. The prisoners and guards occupy a role in Zimbardo's studies; so do passengers. Obedience to pertinent authority figures is something typical passengers share with typical participants in Milgram's studies. And when there is a disturbance on a plane, nonintervention by passengers is not surprising, especially given that such disturbances are matters the airline employees are expected to handle. In the bystander study that I described, participants had no reason to believe that an authority figure (the experimenter) was aware of the apparent emergency. So nonintervention by airplane passengers would seem to be more predictable, other things being equal.

If situations drive behavior in a way that makes new, consciously processed information irrelevant to what we do, then my friend was way too optimistic. But I'm inclined to agree with him. If I had had the horrible misfortune to be on one of the airliners that hit the World Trade Center in 2001, I would probably have refrained from intervening and hoped the airline employees would handle things. In light of what I subsequently learned, I predict that my reactions would be different now. My expectation is that if a passenger or two took action, others would join in.

This last remark is a window on my optimism. Behavioral education starts at an early age. Parents try to teach their toddlers to control potentially harmful impulses, and they enjoy a considerable measure of success. Parents also teach respect for parental authority and they engage in moral education, which also involves instruction in self-control. Of course, parents can only teach what they are familiar with. And a lot more is known now about factors that influence human behavior than was known even a few decades ago. In my view, this knowledge should be put to good use, and not only in child rearing.

Lots of people find striking "news" about human behavior interesting—articles claiming that neuroscientists have shown that free will is an illusion, for example. The classic situationist studies that I have described aren't news now, of course, but they continue to be cited in new studies on situationism or automaticity. One way to spin news about these studies is pessimistic. For example, being in a group that witnesses an emergency has an enormous effect on your behavior, and there is nothing you can do about it. Another way to spin the news is not so pessimistic: now that you know about the bystander effect, you have a better chance of resisting your inclination to remain passive the next time you find yourself in a group that witnesses an emergency. Here we see two very different takes on the same findings.

There are plenty of self-help books on self-control. People learn techniques for resisting or avoiding temptation with a view to making their lives better. People who read such books know what they want to avoid—binge eating, uncontrolled gambling, excessive drinking, or whatever it may be—and they try to learn how to avoid it. When a cause of harmful behavior flies under everyone's radar, not much can be done about it. But once a cause of harmful action or inaction is brought to light, prospects for amelioration may become brighter.

A public that is educated about the bystander effect is less likely to display it. The same is true of undue or excessive obedience to authority. Obedience to authority is important for civil society. Because it's useful, it's instilled by parents, teachers, and others. It becomes habitual in many people. But we also know the evils to which it can lead. Milgram's work was motivated partly by a desire to understand how ordinary German citizens who became rank-and-file military personnel ended up committing atrocities. Obedience to authority is an important part of his answer. The official demand for obedience to authority should include education about proper limits to obedience. Milgram writes: "In growing up, the normal individual has learned to check the expression of aggressive impulses. But the culture has failed, almost entirely, in inculcating internal controls on actions that have their origin in authority. For this reason, the latter constitutes a far greater danger to human survival" (1974, p. 147). Education can lessen this danger.

What about Zimbardo's findings? They have obvious implications for the training of prison guards, and the implications extend to people whose jobs give them considerable power over others—police, for example. But the import of his findings extends much further. There are situations in which continuing to play whatever role we're playing at the time—passenger, army private, student—will handicap us. Knowing about the risk can make it less difficult for us to shed our roles when the time is right.

John Kihlstrom reports that some of his fellow social psychologists "embrace and promote the idea that automatic processes dominate human experience, thought, and action to the virtual exclusion of everything else" (2008, p. 168). If he's exaggerating, he's not exaggerating much. But remember what I said about implementation intentions in Chapter 4. The research discussed there provides evidence that conscious intentions (or their neural correlates) do important work. It counters the impression that, as science correspondent Sandra Blakeslee put it in a *New York Times* article, "in navigating the world and deciding what is rewarding, humans are closer to zombies than sentient beings much of the time" (as quoted in Kihlstrom 2008, p. 163).

Some of Milgram's descriptions of the excessively obedient behavior he observed are similar to descriptions of actions that display what philosophers call "weakness of will," a phenomenon that fascinated Socrates, Plato, and Aristotle long ago and continues to be a lively research topic. Your "weak-willed" actions are avoidable actions that are contrary to your better judgment. A case in point might be eating a second helping of dessert when you believe you shouldn't. Presumably, if no one was holding a gun to your head and you didn't have an irresistible craving, you could have rejected the dessert. Milgram says that "some subjects were totally convinced of the wrongness of what they were doing" (1974, p. 10), and many subjects who continued shocking made "the intellectual decision that they should not give any more shocks" (p. 148). If, in fact, they were capable of abandoning their role as shock-givers, these people were acting in a weak-willed way.

The flip side of weak-willed action is action that exhibits self-control in the face of pressure to act contrary to one's better judgment. The large body of work on implementation intentions affirms that we can indeed exercise self-control and opposes the idea that conscious intentions have virtually no effect on intentional action.

Research on implementation intentions certainly suggests that one useful technique for overcoming anticipated motivation not to do what you judge it best to do later—for example, exercise next week or finish writing a resume by the end of the day—is simply to decide, shortly after making the judgment, on a very specific plan for so doing. Of course, what works against relatively modest motivational opposition might not work when the opposition is considerably stronger.

I'm not suggesting that implementation intentions provide a solution to the problems encountered by participants in the classic studies of situationism. I have simply been providing some support for my optimism about human prospects for self-control and some grounds for not being overly impressed by the aforementioned zombie hypothesis about human beings. The key to dealing with the bystander effect, excessive obedience, and the power of roles is education. Sometimes, knowledge is power.

Even so, the classic situationist studies are disconcerting. One response is pessimism about human agency: some people may conclude that intentional human action is driven primarily by forces that fly under the radar of consciousness and that we have little insight into why we do what we do. Not only have I discussed some evidence to the contrary, but I also have pointed to some merits of an optimistic view according to which knowledge about situational influences can enable human beings to deal rationally with them.

In earlier chapters, I offered straightforward formulations of scientific arguments for the nonexistence of free will. That's harder to do here, because it's harder to see exactly what the argument is supposed to be. Consider the following argument:

Bold situationist argument in a nutshell

1. Human behavior is entirely driven by the situations in which people find themselves and the effects these situations have on automatic behavior-producing processes.
2. If premise 1 is true, no one has free will.
3. So no one has free will.

In Zimbardo's Stanford prison experiment, as in Milgram's experiments and the bystander study, people's situations had a remarkable influence on their behavior. What happened to the guards is very interesting. We can see how an ordinary college student who has the power to do so might be tempted to make someone wash a toilet with his bare hands. But is the temptation irresistible? Obviously, the guards who made prisoners do this *should* have resisted the temptation. And why should it be denied that they could have resisted it? Even though they didn't resist it, they might have been free to resist. The guards' situation in this experiment made it easier for them to make out-of-bounds decisions—decisions about how to use their newfound power. But I don't see that their situation *compelled* them to act as they did. They were not left with no other option. As I see it, it was still to some extent up to them whether they put their inhumane ideas into action or not. After all, many of the guards did not engage in cruel behavior, even if they were tempted to do so. Are we to believe that it was simply impossible for the worse guards to behave like their better colleagues?

Someone may claim that everything we do is completely determined by the situations in which we find ourselves, that we have no control at all over how we respond to these situations, and that the bad guards therefore couldn't have acted differently. The claim is off-base. If situations really did completely determine behavior, then everyone in the same situation would act the same way. But only some of the guards acted cruelly; others didn't. This pessimistic view of decisions isn't true to the facts.

What about the prisoners? Why would they do disgusting things they were commanded to do rather than refusing? Were they *unable* to refuse?

Suppose a guard had ordered a prisoner to stab a fellow prisoner. Would he do it? Or would a command like that bring the prisoner back to reality, just as Zimbardo's reminder about the real world did for the young man who was having a breakdown? If the prisoners can exit their role, their situation doesn't deprive them of free will.

In Milgram's experiment, participants believed they were hurting the learner, and they went on to cause apparent pain anyway. Should we expect similar behavior of a prisoner ordered to stab another prisoner? An important fact shouldn't be overlooked: a convincing authority figure told Milgram's participants that although the shocks can be very painful, they would not cause any permanent tissue damage. But because Zimbardo's prisoners *knew* that stabbing someone would cause serious tissue damage, I don't believe they would have gone that far. They would have snapped back to reality and disobeyed the guard.

Return to the bystander experiment. Would you say that the participants who believed that other people were around to help had no control at all over their own decisions? It's normal to be at least a little confused about what to do in a strange emergency situation like that. When the participants think that four other people are around to help, they might assume that one of them is likely to have a better grip on what to do. Even so, the right thing to do is to run for help. They've got to know that, even if it takes them a little while to realize it. Recall, however, that about 70 percent of the people who thought they were in the large group *didn't* do that—at least during the two minutes that they heard the frantic voice. That's disturbing, but I wouldn't conclude that they didn't have free will at the time, or that they weren't free to run for help. They made a bad decision—and possibly made it freely. I see no good reason to deny that they *could have* done what the other 30 percent actually did.

Believing four other people are around to help evidently makes it more difficult to make the right decision, but it doesn't make it impossible. About a third of the participants do make the right decision, after all. I'd say the participants in this experiment aren't total victims of their situation. They're influenced but not determined by their situations.

In the same vein, a significant percentage of Milgram's participants stop shocking the learner, despite the experimenter's instructions to continue. If behavior were driven entirely by situations, then all Milgram's participants would have behaved the same way. (They were all in the same situation, after all.) But they didn't.

If you think that having free will requires being totally free from situational influences, you should conclude that there's no free will. But let's be realistic. People are significantly influenced by their situations— and more so than you probably thought. The question is whether, even so, they sometimes have enough control over what they do to act of their own free will. What do you think? Keep in mind that even if you're never a subject in a scientific experiment, being in a bystander situation is a realistic possibility. So, if you saw a young woman being assaulted on a busy street or an old man slip and fall in a crowded mall, would it be up to you to some extent whether you tried to help? The situationist experimental findings fall far short of proving that it wouldn't be. And knowing what you do about the bystander effect, you might make a special effort to step up to the plate and take control of the situation! Knowledge is power. Forewarned is forearmed.

6 | FREE WILL AND EVIDENCE

A few years ago, at the World Science Festival, neuro-scientist Patrick Haggard, psychologist Daniel Wegner, and I—under the direction of moderator Paul Nurse—chatted about free will in front of a large, enthusiastic audience at the 92nd Street Y in New York City. A *New York Times* article on the session inspired many bloggers. Some of them said they believed in free will; others took the opposite position, sometimes citing scientific studies as support. Most of them sounded very confident. I was struck by the variety of different ways in which the bloggers seemed to understand the expression "free will." To some, free will had to be utterly magical or absolutely unconstrained. Others thought of free will in a very down-to-earth way. And as you might expect, whether the bloggers affirmed or denied the existence of free will tended to vary with how high they set the bar for it.

Where different people set the bar for free will is an issue I come back to later in this chapter. It's intertwined with the issue of evidence for and against free will, a central issue in this chapter.

What is the evidence for the existence of free will? That depends on what you mean by "free will." In Chapter 1, I sketched three different conceptions of free will. Because a discussion of evidence for or against the existence of souls is beyond my range, I'll concentrate on the two conceptions that don't invoke souls.

According to one conception, having the ability to make—and act on the basis of—rational, informed decisions when you're not being subjected to undue force is sufficient for having free will. This was the free-will analogue of regular gas in Chapter 1. Let's call it *modest free will*. Most of us certainly seem to have this ability at least some of the time. And it seems that we sometimes display this ability in making decisions of the kind at issue and acting accordingly. Your own life provides you with evidence that this ability is sometimes at work in you and in people you interact with. I have described some arguments to the effect that scientific discoveries have undermined this evidence of yours. But I also have explained why the scientific findings are not all they are cracked up to be.

Some readers may believe that free will requires what I called *deep openness*. They say that we must add something important to the modest conception of free will. What must be added, they insist, is that free agents have open to them alternative decisions that are compatible with everything that has already happened and with the laws of nature. Let's call the result *ambitious free will*. It was associated with mid-grade gas in Chapter 1's gas station analogy.

Discussions of ambitious free will can quickly get very technical. I'll try to avoid technicality here. Earlier this week, a friend of mine was asked to serve as a volunteer bartender at a fundraising event. Sometimes she says yes to such requests and sometimes no. Relevant factors include how busy she is, her level of interest in the cause being promoted, and how much volunteer work she's done recently. On this occasion she decided to say yes. Now, imagine that time (and the whole universe, actually) could be rewound in something like the way you rewind a movie you are watching on your favorite media player. And imagine that, after my friend made her decision, time was rewound to a moment just before she decided to say yes. Everything is exactly the same as it was the first time through. But this time, as things go forward, what happens next is that she decides to say no. This is a way to picture deep openness. If my friend had deep openness at the time she made her decision, then if time could be rewound again and again for just a few moments, she'd make different decisions in some of the replays.

Do we have evidence that ambitious free will exists? You might think it's obvious that we do. When we're unsure about what to do and mulling the matter over, it feels like more than one decision is open to us. But what would it feel like if, in fact, alternative decisions *weren't* open to us in the deep way required by ambitious free will? What would it feel like if, given the way our universe and everything in it works (including us), an imaginary super-computer provided with complete information about the laws of nature and a complete description of the universe many years ago could deduce everything we will decide? What would it feel like if it were *necessarily* true that, given the laws of nature and the condition of our universe at some past time, we proceed to make each and every decision we've actually made so far, in exactly the way we made them, and with the feelings we had at the time?

The answer, to the best of my knowledge, is this: just the way it normally feels, just the way things feel now. I'm not saying that we don't have deep openness. I'm saying that the difference between deep openness and its absence isn't the kind of thing that can be *felt*. We sometimes do feel uncertain about what we will do. But we can have exactly that feeling even if someone who has access to the imaginary computer's deductions is certain about what we will do. Your not knowing what you will decide is one thing; having deep openness regarding what you will decide is another.

I can't *taste* the difference between Coke and Pepsi. And, as I see it, no one can *feel* the difference between deep openness and its absence. Now, there are other ways for me to get evidence about whether a cola someone poured in a glass is Coke or Pepsi (or something else). And there may be ways, at least in principle, to get evidence about whether we have or lack deep openness. I'm certainly not saying that it's impossible to discover whether deep openness exists. My claim is only that the discovery won't be made by attending to how things feel to us.

So is there hard evidence of deep openness? Some scientists say they've found evidence of something like it in fruit flies (Brembs 2011). If a fruit fly turned to the left a moment ago and time were wound backward a couple of moments, it might turn to the right in the rerun. There's no evidence that fruit flies have free will. Instead, there's evidence that something that some people regard as necessary for free will—behavior-producing processes that aren't deterministic—is present in fruit flies. And if such processes are present in them, they might be part of our evolutionary heritage; they might be present in us too.

Take a huge leap from tiny animals to the entire universe. According to leading interpretations of quantum mechanics, genuine chance is built into the fabric of the universe. If a certain photon veered left a moment ago and time were wound backward a couple of moments, that photon might veer right in the rerun. For all we know, the universe and our brains leave room for deep openness and ambitious free will.

The experiments I've discussed in this book don't rule out the existence of modest free will, as I have explained. So the only way for these experiments to rule out the existence of its ambitious counterpart is to prove that the extra element—deep openness—doesn't exist. Someone might think the neuroscience experiments I described prove that the brain works deterministically with no room for deep openness. But, as I hope I've convinced you by now, the experiments prove no such thing. Even the most impressive success rate at predicting what participants would do on the basis of brain readings was 80 percent. Here we have probabilities. So we have something that's compatible with the brain *not* working deterministically.

Is there hard evidence that our brains work indeterministically in the way they'd need to if we have deep openness? Is there evidence that sometimes, right up to the moment of decision, there really are different important possibilities for what happens next in the brain? I haven't seen convincing evidence of this one way or the other. The issue is still open. Human brains are enormously complicated. It would be extremely difficult—and certainly not possible today—to control experimental conditions so you could tell that a brain event wasn't determined by anything and was partly a matter of chance.

If my physicist friends are right, the clicks of a Geiger counter—a handheld device that detects the emission of nuclear radiation—are caused by something that's not deterministically caused, that is, the decay of particles of certain kinds. Suppose that's right about what happens out there in the world. How do we know that once the sound waves hit the eardrums things don't go deterministic in the brain? Maybe we don't. But we don't know that things *do* go deterministic there either.

Even ambitious free will is a live option. Science has not closed the door on it. So why do some scientists say that free will is an illusion?

When I'm asked whether I believe in free will, I start by saying that it depends on what you mean by "free will." Suppose Jeff asks me whether resident aliens exist. I'm thinking about people like my friend Flori, a Romanian citizen living in the United States. So I say yes. But he's thinking about beings from other planets who reside on Earth. So he infers that I believe in the existence of such beings. Sometimes it's important to say what we mean by an expression before we make claims about existence.

Over the past decade, the idea that scientists have proved that free will is an illusion has received a lot of press. Do the scientists who claim this mean pretty much the same thing by "free will" as most readers of the news reports? Let's take a look at what some of the scientists who contend that free will is an illusion say about the meaning of "free will."

In a 2008 article in *Current Biology*, Read Montague writes:

> Free will is the idea that we make choices and have thoughts independent of anything remotely resembling a physical process. Free will is the close cousin to the idea of the soul—the concept that "you," your thoughts and feelings, derive from an entity that is separate and distinct from the physical mechanisms that make up your body. From this perspective, your choices are not caused by physical events, but instead emerge wholly formed from somewhere indescribable and outside the purview of physical descriptions. This implies that free will cannot have evolved by natural selection, as that would place it directly in a stream of causally connected events. (p. 584)

This picture of free will is distinctly magical.

Biologist Anthony Cashmore asserts in a 2010 article that "if we no longer entertain the luxury of a belief in the 'magic of the soul,' then there is little else to offer in support of the concept of free will" (p. 4499). He goes on, writing: "In the absence of any molecular model accommodating the concept of free will, I have to conclude that the dualism of Descartes is alive and well. That is, just like Descartes, we still believe (much as we pretend otherwise) that there is a magic component to human behavior" (p. 4503).

In his 2011 book, *Who's in Charge? Free Will and the Science of the Brain*, neuroscientist Michael Gazzaniga says that free will involves a ghostly or nonphysical element and "some secret stuff that is YOU" (p. 108). Obviously, this isn't a report of a scientific discovery about what "free will" means; he's telling us how he understands that expression— that is, what "free will" means to him. The same is true of Montague and Cashmore, who tell us what *they* mean by this expression. Given what Gazzaniga means by "free will," it's no surprise that, in his view, "free will is a miscast concept, based on social and psychological beliefs...that have not been borne out and/or are at odds with modern scientific knowledge about the nature of our universe" (p. 219).

The overwhelming majority of philosophy professors who write about free will these days do not see it as magical, supernatural, or unnatural. They would reject as outlandish the descriptions of free will offered by Montague, Cashmore, and Gazzaniga.

If a philosophy professor and a biology professor who disagree about what "free will" means were having a cordial discussion about their disagreement, it would not be surprising if, before long, one of them said that the other was using the expression in a specialized way that is out of touch with ordinary usage. Now, biologists know that the simple fact that they are biologists doesn't give them any special insight into what the expression "free will" means. (Some biologists may believe that philosophers don't have any special insight into its meaning either, and they may offer as evidence the fact that philosophers disagree with each other on this topic.) Biologists can be led to entertain the thought that their understanding of that expression may be an artifact of their own personal upbringing and to consider the hypothesis that they are out of touch with ordinary usage of "free will." In experiments with human participants, scientists definitely prefer to have a sample size larger than one person, and any scientist can see that if the way he or she goes about determining what "free will" means is simply to consult his or her own feeling or intuition about the meaning, then—to the extent to which it is important to avoid being mistaken about the meaning of "free will"—he or she should seek a better method. (The simple, navel-gazing method is not recommended for philosophers either, of course.)

The imaginary discussion between the pair of professors might grind to a halt, with neither professor giving any ground. If that happens, should the professors just agree to disagree and part company? Should they instead look for an arbitrator who is neither a biologist nor a philosopher? If so, where should they turn?

Here's an idea. There's an interesting body of work in psychology and experimental philosophy on what non-specialists mean by "free will." It uses survey studies, and thousands of people have now been surveyed. If our imaginary discussants were to look into this work, they would discover that much of it supports the idea that the bold claims about the meaning of "free will" that I have quoted from Montague, Cashmore, and Gazzaniga are accepted only by a minority of people. (To interested readers, I recommend Mele 2012, Monroe and Malle 2010, and Nahmias and Thompson 2014) For example, even if lots of people believe in souls, there is considerable evidence that many of them do not regard free will as something that depends on the existence of souls. It looks as though Montague, Cashmore, and Gazzaniga are setting the bar for free will way higher than most people do. And, as I explained, the reason they set it so high doesn't come from science. Instead, they're simply telling us what they themselves happen to mean by the words *free will*.

I asked why some scientists say that free will doesn't exist. Here's a short answer: because they set the bar for free will ridiculously high. It's a simple fact that you can argue that something—anything at all—doesn't exist by setting the bar for its existence extremely high. Let's look at an example. Bob claims that there have never been any great baseball players—that the existence of great baseball players is an illusion. When I ask him to explain, he says that a great baseball player would need to have a batting average of at least .400 for at least twenty consecutive seasons, pitch at least ten perfect games, and hit a minimum of two thousand home runs; he correctly reports that no one has ever come anywhere close to this incredible performance. If that is what it takes to be a great baseball player, then no great baseball players have ever existed and Bob has made his point. But most of us who are interested in baseball set the bar for greatness far lower, and we are not at all embarrassed about doing so. Babe Ruth and Willie Mays were great baseball players, and so were a host of others. Bob's requirements for greatness are ridiculously excessive.

Where should we set the bar for free will? That's an interesting question, to be sure, and one that philosophers have argued about for a very long time. The point I want to make is that the higher one sets the bar, the more likely one is to see free will as an illusion. Here are two different high bars: 1) having free will requires making conscious choices that are entirely independent of preceding brain activity, and 2) having free will requires being absolutely unconstrained by genetics and environment (including the situations in which we find ourselves). Now, there is excellent evidence that our conscious choices are never entirely independent of preceding brain activity and that we are not absolutely unconstrained by genetics and environment. But this evidence threatens the existence of free will only if the bar for free will is set absurdly high.

A good way to tether our thinking about free will to the real world is to view it as something we need in order to deserve moral credit or moral blame for some of our actions. If we think about free will this way, then to the extent to which it strikes us as plausible that people sometimes deserve—from a moral point of view—credit or blame for what they do, we should also find it plausible that people sometimes exercise free will. Thinking about free will in terms of what important uses it might have tends to curb enthusiasm for setting the bar at dizzying heights.

It's interesting that although Gazzaniga rejects free will as magical and contrary to science, he takes a very different view of responsibility and accountability. "There is no scientific reason not to hold people accountable and responsible," he writes (2011, p. 106). Someone might say that it's a good idea to *hold* people responsible even if they aren't in fact responsible, but Gazzaniga isn't advocating that idea. Evidently, he sets a much lower bar for responsibility than for free will. But, as I have said, he has no scientific grounds for setting the bar for free will where he does. Nothing that comes from science prevents him from lowering his bar for free will to bring it into line with his bar for responsibility. If he were to do that, he might start saying that there is no scientific reason to believe that free will is an illusion!

I must confess that discussing scientific challenges to the existence of free will in general terms makes me uncomfortable. I believe that properly discussing such challenges requires describing the experiments that supposedly show that free will is an illusion and explaining why they miss their mark. The general structure of these arguments is simple, as you have seen. In stage 1, data are offered in support of some featured empirical proposition, for example, the proposition that conscious intentions are never among the causes of corresponding actions. In stage 2, the featured empirical proposition is combined with a proposition that expresses some aspect of the author's view about what "free will" means, yielding the conclusion that free will does not exist. One conclusion I argued for in earlier chapters is that the data do not justify various empirical propositions featured in these arguments. If my arguments are successful, the scientific arguments are shown to be unsuccessful even before there is any need to examine claims about what "free will" means.

There are people—including some philosophers— who say that modest free will isn't really free will; it's too modest. Some readers may agree with them while others disagree. In my writing on free will, I've always been officially neutral on this issue. But I've argued (in *Autonomous Agents* and in *Free Will and Luck*) that the claim that free will exists is more credible than the claim that it doesn't. In a more recent book, *Effective Intentions* (2009), I've argued that this position of mine isn't undermined by the allegedly most threatening scientific discoveries—discoveries that are supposed to show that free will is an illusion. I've argued for the same thing in this book. If there is an illusion in the neighborhood, it's the illusion that there's strong scientific evidence for the nonexistence of free will.

So, you ask, does free will exist? If you mean what I call *modest free will*, I say yes without hesitation. If you mean what I call *ambitious free will*, I say the jury is still out. In fact, this point about the jury is the main moral of this book. Scientists most definitely have not proved that free will—even ambitious free will—is an illusion. For all we know now, ambitious free will is widespread. If it isn't, at least modest free will is.

REFERENCES

Baumeister, R., E. Masicampo, and C. DeWall. 2009. "Prosocial Benefits of Feeling Free: Disbelief in Free Will Increases Aggression and Reduces Helpfulness." *Personality and Social Psychology Bulletin* 35: 260–68.

Brembs, B. 2011. "Towards a Scientific Concept of Free Will as a Biological Trait: Spontaneous Actions and Decision-Making in Invertebrates." *Proceedings of the Royal Society Biological Sciences* 278: 930–39.

Cashmore, A. 2010. "The Lucretian Swerve: The Biological Basis of Human Behavior and the Criminal Justice System." *Proceedings of the National Academy of Sciences of the United States of America* 107: 4499–504.

Darley, J., and B. Latané. 1968. "Bystander Intervention in Emergencies: Diffusion of Responsibility." *Journal of Personality and Social Psychology* 8: 377–83.

Dweck, C., and D. Molden. 2008. "Self-Theories: The Construction of Free Will." In *Are We Free? Psychology and Free Will*. Edited by J. Baer, J. Kaufman, and R. Baumeister. New York: Oxford University Press.

Fried, I., R. Mukamel, and G. Kreiman. 2011. "Internally Generated Preactivation of Single Neurons in Human Medial Frontal Cortex Predicts Volition." *Neuron* 69: 548–62.

Gazzaniga, M. 2011. *Who's in Charge? Free Will and the Science of the Brain*. New York: HarperCollins.

Gollwitzer, P. 1999. "Implementation Intentions." *American Psychologist* 54: 493–503.

Gollwitzer, P., and P. Sheeran. 2006. "Implementation Intentions and Goal Achievement: A Meta-Analysis of Effects and Processes." *Advances in Experimental Social Psychology* 38: 69–119.

Haggard, P., and E. Magno. 1999. "Localising Awareness of Action with Transcranial Magnetic Stimulation." *Experimental Brain Research* 127: 102–7.

Haney, C., W. Banks, and P. Zimbardo. 1973. "Interpersonal Dynamics of a Simulated Prison." *International Journal of Criminology and Penology* 1: 69–97.

Kihlstrom, J. 2008. "The Automaticity Juggernaut—or Are We Automatons After All?" In *Are We Free? Psychology and Free Will*. Edited by J. Baer, J. Kaufman, and R. Baumeister. New York: Oxford University Press.

Libet, B. 1985. "Unconscious Cerebral Initiative and the Role of Conscious Will in Voluntary Action." *Behavioral and Brain Sciences* 8: 529–66.

Libet, B. 2004. *Mind Time*. Cambridge, MA: Harvard University Press.

Mele, A. 1995. *Autonomous Agents*. New York: Oxford University Press.

Mele, A. 2006. *Free Will and Luck*. New York: Oxford University Press.

Mele, A. 2009. *Effective Intentions*. New York: Oxford University Press.

Mele, A. 2012. "Another Scientific Threat to Free Will?" *Monist* 95: 422–40.

Milgram, S. 1963. "Behavioral Study of Obedience." *The Journal of Abnormal and Social Psychology* 67: 371–78.

Milgram, S. 1974. *Obedience to Authority*. New York: Harper & Row.

Monroe, A., and B. Malle. 2010. "From Uncaused Will to Conscious Choice: The Need to Study, Not Speculate About People's Folk

Concept of Free Will." *Review of Philosophy and Psychology* 1: 211–24.

Montague, P. R. 2008. "Free Will." *Current Biology* 18: R584–85.

Nahmias, E., and M. Thompson. 2014 "A Naturalistic Vision of Free Will." In *Current Controversies in Experimental Philosophy*. Edited by E. O'Neill and E. Machery. Boston: Routledge.

Ramachandran, V. 2004. *A Brief Tour of Human Consciousness*. New York: Pi Press.

Soon, C. S., M. Brass, H. J. Heinze, and J. D. Haynes. 2008. "Unconscious Determinants of Free Decisions in the Human Brain." *Nature Neuroscience*. 11: 543–45.

Vohs, K., and J. Schooler. 2008. "The Value of Believing in Free Will: Encouraging a Belief in Determinism Increases Cheating." *Psychological Science* 19: 49–54.

Wegner, D. 2002. *The Illusion of Conscious Will*. Cambridge, MA: MIT Press.

Youngsteadt, E. 2008. "Case Closed for Free Will?" *ScienceNOW Daily News*. April 14.

Zimbardo, P. n.d. "Stanford Prison Experiment." http://www.prison-exp.org.

Zimbardo, P., C. Haney, W. Banks, and D. Jaffe. 1973. "The Mind Is a Formidable Jailer: A Pirandellian Prison." *The New York Times Magazine*, Section 6, April 8: 38–60.

INDEX